How do I us

Key Words with Peter an
parallel series, each containin
series are written using the same carefully controlled
vocabulary. Readers will get the most out of **Key Words** with
Peter and Jane when they follow the books in the pattern
1a, 1b, 1c; 2a, 2b, 2c and so on.

• Series a
gradually introduces and repeats new words.

• Series b
provides further practice of these same words, but
in a different context and with different illustrations.

• Series c
uses familiar words to teach **phonics** in a methodical way,
enabling children to read increasingly difficult words.
It also provides a link to writing.

Published by Ladybird Books Ltd
A Penguin Company
Penguin Books Ltd , 80 Strand, London WC2R 0RL, UK
Penguin Books Australia Ltd, 707 Collins Street, Melbourne, Victoria 3008, Australia
Penguin Group (NZ) 67 Apollo Drive, Rosedale, North Shore 0632, New Zealand

019

ISBN: 978-1-40930-148-6

Printed in China

Key Words

with Peter and Jane

9a

Games we like

written by W. Murray
illustrated by M. Aitchison

The boy and the girl in the shop are our friends Peter and Jane. They have come to buy some toys. There are many toys in the shop, and the children take some time to find what they want.

The man in the shop helps them. He finds a skipping rope for Jane, and another long rope for Peter.

Then Peter tells him that he wants a gun. As the man goes to get a gun, Peter and his sister look at the balloons.

Jane takes red, white, yellow and green balloons from the box. "We will have all these," she says.

They look at the books next. Peter has a book about trains, and Jane finds the scrapbooks she wants. They are big scrapbooks.

The man comes back. He has found a gun. "Thank you," says Peter, as he gives the man his money.

The children go home with their toys. Jane has the balloons, the skipping rope and the scrapbooks. Peter has his long rope, his book and the gun.

5

Peter and Jane show their friends the things they have bought. First they look at the balloons, then the scrapbooks and the book about trains.

The two girls use the skipping rope, and the two boys play with the gun.

Jane can skip very well. She skips quickly. Then her friend has a turn. She can skip quickly, too.

Peter has the gun. He shows his friend how it shoots. There is no danger. The gun shoots a little white ball. It shoots a long way. First Peter shoots with the gun, and then his friend has a turn. "I am glad you bought this, Peter," he says.

The girls watch the boys as they shoot with the gun. Then the boys show them how to use it, and the girls have a turn.

After this the boys play with the skipping rope. Peter can skip, and so can his friend.

"We can't skip as quickly as the girls," says Peter, "but I don't think the girls can shoot as well as we can."

7

The children blow up the balloons that they have bought.

Mary has a green balloon, and Jane has a yellow one. Mary blows hers up until it is very big. Jane blows up her yellow balloon and then paints a face on it. "Come and look at this face, Mary," she says. "Come and watch me paint."

Peter has a white balloon. He blows his up, and then sees Jane's. "I will paint a face, too," he says.

As Peter paints he calls out to Bob, "Come and look at this, Bob. It has a face like yours."

But Bob does not come. He has lost his red balloon. He has let it go, and it is going quickly up and up. He thinks that it won't come down.

He calls to the others, "I have lost my balloon. I can't get it. It is going over the trees, and it won't come down." He does not know what to do.

Jane says, "If you can't get it back we will give you another one."

The girls take turns to skip with the skipping rope Jane has bought.

The boys play Cowboys and Indians. Bob has Indian clothes and a gun. There is paint on his face. Peter has cowboy clothes. He has his gun and a long rope.

Today the Indian and the cowboy are friends. Peter shows Bob how to use his rope, and then Bob the Indian shows Peter the cowboy how to shoot with his gun. It uses caps. Nothing comes out of it when he shoots, so there is no danger.

They see the red balloon in the tree. Bob tries to get the balloon down with the rope. He throws the rope at the balloon but he can't hit it. Peter tries to shoot it down with his gun. He hits the balloon with a little white ball, but it does not come down.

Then the boys throw sticks at the balloon. Peter throws and Bob throws, but the balloon does not come down.

At last a stick hits the red balloon and down it comes.

When the weather is fine the children like to be out in the garden. It is a fine day today and Peter and Jane are going to play a game with Bob and Mary.

"Let us have a fight," says Peter. "The cowboy and the cowgirl can fight the Indians."

"Mary and I won't play if you fight," says Jane. "We can't fight and we don't want to be hurt."

"You won't get hurt," says Peter. "It is only a game. Come on, it will be fun."

Then the girls say that they will play. Mary tries to look like an Indian girl. She has Indian clothes, and paint on her face.

Jane tries to look like a cowgirl. She has on cowgirl's clothes. "You look just like a cowgirl," says Peter. "Let us climb into the tree."

The cowboy and the cowgirl climb quickly into the house in the tree. They are going to shoot out of the window at the Indians.

Indian Bob climbs the tree. He is by the window. Mary the Indian girl is by the door.

It is a fine day again. The children have put up the tent in the garden. They pretend it is a hospital tent. They are going to play a game called Doctors and Nurses.

Peter has on his cowboy clothes. He pretends he has been hurt in a fight with the Indians.

Mary and Bob pretend to be nurses in the hospital. They help Peter to climb onto the bed.

Peter tells the nurses that he has been in a fight with some Indians. He pretends that he has hurt his arm. The nurses look at his arm.

"We must get the Doctor at once," says Nurse Bob. He goes quickly out of the tent.

"I will look after you," says Nurse Mary. "The other nurse will get the Doctor."

In comes Jane. She pretends to be the Doctor of the hospital. She talks to Cowboy Peter and looks at his arm.

"We can make your arm better," the Doctor says, "but you must be in hospital for some time, so that we can look after you."

Sometimes the children like to use their scrap-books. They like to put photographs and pictures in these books. Sometimes they write in the scrapbooks.

Their Dad has been taking photographs of them for a long time. Some are very good. Soon he is going to show both the children how to take photographs.

Jane laughs as she looks at the photograph she holds. In it she has on one of Mum's hats. She shows it to Peter, and he laughs, too.

Peter laughs at another photograph. In this one he holds the donkey as Jane puts her hat on its head. She holds her doll on its back for a ride.

Now Jane looks at a picture she has made. In it she is a beautiful queen. "This is a lovely one," she says. "I will put it in the book."

Peter looks out of the window. "The sun is out now," he says. "It is a lovely day."

The children put the scrapbooks away and go out in the sun to play.

Daddy has bought a little camera. It takes photographs in colour. He shows the camera to Jane and Peter and lets them hold it.

"I am glad the photographs will be in colour," says Jane. "Colour makes the pictures pretty."

"I like colour better than black and white," says Peter. "Can I use the camera sometimes?" he asks his father. He wants to take pictures by himself.

"I would like to use it sometimes, as well," says Jane.

Daddy laughs. He tells the children that he has bought the camera for them to use. But he says that he must use it first himself, to learn how to work it. Then he will show them how to take photographs.

They go into the garden, so that Daddy can take some photographs.

"You pick some of those pretty flowers by the wall," Daddy says to Jane. "It will make a pretty picture."

As Jane goes over to the flowers a butterfly comes by her. "Good," she says. "Its lovely colour will look nice in the photograph.'

Here is Jane, with the camera. She is taking a colour photograph of her brother. She likes taking pictures by herself and without anyone to help her. At first Dad had to show her how to hold the camera and also tell her what to do. Then she could use it by herself.

Peter can also use the camera, and has been taking photographs without anyone to help him.

Bob and Mary look over the wall to see what is going on. Then they climb over. Peter and Jane show their two friends their new camera and tell them all about it. They show them some photographs.

"They are pretty," says Mary. "I wish I had a camera to take colour photographs like this."

"You can use this one sometimes," says Jane.

"May I use it now?" asks Bob.

Peter says that he can, and so the children take more photographs. They laugh and have fun as they use the camera.

Father looks out of the window. He is glad he bought the camera for the children.

It is a fine day again, and the boys are going off together to make a camp in the woods. They are taking their tea to eat in their camp. Jane asks if she can come.

"Of course you can," says Peter. "Bring Mary also, or she will be by herself, and she won't like that."

Pat runs out with the children as they all go off together. "Good old Pat," says Peter. "Of course you must come. We can't go without you."

When they get to the woods Peter shows them how to make the camp. He tells the others that they want lots of sticks to make the walls.

"We also want plenty of grass," he says.

Peter and Bob go off to get the sticks and Jane and Mary get some grass. Men have been at work in the woods and there are lots of sticks there.

"Let us do the work first," says Peter. "Then we can have our tea."

They sing as they work together. They are all happy.

The children are having fun as they work together on the camp.

"Won't it be dark inside?" asks Mary. "We can't see in the dark."

"Yes, of course it will be dark inside if we don't make a door and a window," says Peter. "We will make them now."

After this Peter gets some more sticks and grass to make the roof. He climbs up a tree so that he can make the roof.

Bob helps Peter to make the roof out of the sticks and grass. Then they put grass inside the camp on the floor, and get a big log to sit on.

They like having their tea inside the camp. They sit on the log and on the floor, and talk about the games they will play.

"This is just the place to play Cowboys and Indians," says Peter. "The next time we play that, I want to be the Indian. Bob can be the cowboy."

"Yes," says Mary, "I'll be the cowgirl this time, and Jane can be the Indian girl."

The children are in the woods, having fun. They go on through the woods, to explore.

Peter and Jane know where there is an old empty house by the woods. Nobody has lived in it for very many years. "Let us go to the empty house," says Peter. "Bob and Mary have never been there. It would be fun to explore it with them."

When they come to the empty house they see that the door is open. They look through the door and see that it is dark inside.

They all go in to explore the rooms. "There is nobody here," says Peter.

"I think I can hear something," Jane says. "Can't anyone hear it?"

Mary says, "What is it?"

A cat comes out of one of the rooms. It is glad to see them.

"So that is what we could hear," says Jane. "It is one of the cats from the farm. I think she knows us. She knows how to find her way about."

Soon it is time for the children to go back home.

This is a game called Treasure Hunt. You can play it in the house or outside. Many people can play the game together.

The treasure can be a bag of sweets. Someone goes out of the room, and one of the others hides the treasure and some little cards.

The boy or girl who is outside does not know where the treasure or the cards are, but the others know.

Then the boy or girl who is to hunt comes back into the room. Someone gives him a card, and he has to read what is on it. This will tell him where to find another card.

He hunts for this, and when he finds it, he reads what is on it. It will tell him where to find another card. He hunts for this, finds it, and reads where to find another card.

This goes on until he has found all the cards. The last one tells him where to look for the treasure.

He has to read all the cards to find the treasure.

The children are having a game of Treasure Hunt. Peter went outside first. Then someone hid six little cards, and then hid a bag of sweets for the treasure.

All of the six small cards have writing on them.

Peter comes back. Someone tells him that the first card is by the clock. He looks by the clock and finds the card. He reads the writing on it. It says, "On the floor by the door."

He finds the next card on the floor by the door. He looks at the writing on the card. If he can't read it he won't know where to find the next one. Then he won't find the treasure. He has to read the writing by himself. Nobody must tell him.

"This game helps you to learn to read," says Peter.

He reads the writing. It says, "Look by the apples."

Peter goes on with the game to read the writing on all the six small cards. He finds the treasure.

Then Mary goes out for her turn.

Look by
the fire

31

It is raining, so the children play inside today. Peter is blowing bubbles, and Jane is doing the same.

Peter blows six small ones. Some fall on the floor by the dog. He does not know what they are. He wants to eat some but soon finds that he can't.

Jane is blowing a very big bubble. Peter sees this and is soon doing the same himself. "Look at my big one," he says. "Just look at its colours."

"Yes, its colours are beautiful," says Mary. "I can see through it. Let me blow bubbles, too."

Soon all four children are blowing bubbles.

Then it stops raining and they go outside. They go on blowing bubbles and watch them go up and up.

Some of the bubbles go through an open window, and Mrs Green from next door looks out to see where they have come from.

She laughs at the children as they blow bubbles. She knows how they like to do it. She did the same when she was a little girl.

It is a sunny summer day. The children are away at the sea for the day. The sea is not far from where they live. Here they are on the rocks by the sea.

The two girls both sit on the rocks while they watch the boys. Peter and Bob are going to swim under the water.

They are not going far under the water, so there is little danger. The water is not deep. Dad is on the sands not far away. He watches them while he sits in the sun.

Peter goes under first, while the others watch from the rocks. He wants to explore by himself, and swims about for some time. Then he comes up to tell them about it.

"It's not deep," he says. "I saw a fish down there, but it hid by the rocks when it saw me."

Now Peter watches while Bob is doing the same as he did.

When Bob comes up he says, "I saw the fish, but it soon hid by the rocks again."

The sun is in the sky, and it is a warm day. "What a beautiful blue sky," says Jane.

"Yes," says Mary, "and it's so warm."

When the boys come out of the water they ask the girls what they have been doing. The girls tell them that they have been to explore the sands, and to collect interesting things. They have put them on a rock.

"You ought to go under the water," says Peter. "It's very interesting, and the sea is warm. It's not deep, but you ought not to go too far out."

The boys go along the sands to collect some more interesting things. When they come back they put them with the others.

Jane and Mary are in the sea. Mary can swim very well, and she knows how to dive into deep water. Now she swims under the water. Jane does not swim very well.

The boys call the girls to come and see the interesting things they have collected.

"We ought to take these home," says Bob.

The girls find plenty to do when it is raining. It is raining this afternoon, and they are in the house.

Mum has said that they can cook in the kitchen. They can have the kitchen to themselves for the afternoon, to cook what they want. They enjoy being in the kitchen making things themselves.

"First we ought to collect the things we are going to use," says Jane.

When all is ready they make some cakes and other nice things. They enjoy themselves very much.

"I don't know where the boys are, do you?" asks Mary.

Just then the two boys open the kitchen door. "Look, Bob," says Peter. "Here are two cooks in the kitchen. They know how to enjoy themselves, don't they? Are the cakes ready to eat?"

"No, they are not ready," says Jane. She looks at the kitchen clock. "They won't be ready until four o'clock."

"I don't see why boys can't cook things," says Bob. "Will you show us how to cook?"

The children enjoy themselves in the warm kitchen. The girls are going to show the boys how to cook. They want to make real toffee apples. "We will make some real toffee while you boys get the apples ready," says Jane.

Bob gets some sticks for the toffee apples. "Nobody can eat toffee apples without sticks," he says.

Peter brings in eight apples.

"Why eight apples?" asks Mary.

"Two for each of us," says Peter. "Four people with two each makes eight."

"That's what we learn at school," says Bob. "Four twos are eight, and two fours make eight."

The boys put one apple on each stick. Then they watch the girls make the toffee. "It's real toffee, just like you can buy," says Peter.

"Of course it's real," says Mary.

The boys put the apples in the toffee, and eight toffee apples are ready. "Don't forget there are two each," says Peter.

Bob says, "Don't forget the cakes." Jane looks at the clock.

"I won't forget," she says.

41

Peter is making a toy aeroplane. He likes making things with his hands. He thinks it will be interesting to make a toy aeroplane.

He has to fit the parts of the aeroplane together to make it. There is a little book with pictures to show him how to do it. If he fits all the parts together the aeroplane will fly.

Bob comes along and asks Peter what he is making. Peter shows him the parts he has to fit together. Bob asks if he can help. They are making the aeroplane together when Peter's father comes in. They ask him to help, and soon they fit all the parts together.

Then they go outside to fly the aeroplane. It goes up into the sky and then goes round and round. The boys take turns to make the aeroplane fly. They keep it away from the trees.

Dad looks on. He likes to see the boys enjoy themselves.

"This is fun," says Peter to Bob. "I am glad we made the aeroplane."

Jane and Peter are making a model town. Someone has made them a present of a building set. It is a large building set and they both enjoy building with it.

The set has a book with it. This has pictures in it which show how to fit the parts together, and how to make models. It also shows how a model town can be made.

The town has houses and roads. The children put small cars on the roads. To make it more interesting they put in a café and a hospital. There is a car park by the hospital.

Jane says, "We must have a street of shops for the people who live in our model town."

Peter says, "Their children must go to school. We must have a model school." Then he says, "We ought to have a station and a train in it. Let's put them here."

"This is fun," says Jane. "I wish we had little people to put in our model town. I think this is a lovely building set."

The children are having sports. It is just the afternoon for sports, as it is a fine day, but not too hot.

Peter and Bob race against each other. They race against each other three times. Peter wins the first two races and then Bob wins the next race.

Mary and Jane are good at jumping. They like jumping with each other. Mary wins every time. Then Mary and Jane race against each other just as the boys did. It is Jane's turn to win now.

Bob is better than Peter at jumping. They like jumping with one another.

They enjoy their sports, but they get warm as they run and jump. After a while they want to stop, and Peter says he would like an ice-cream.

They go to a shop for some ice-cream, and as they walk along they talk. "Do you know there is to be a sports day at school?" asks Bob.

"Good," says Peter. "I think we will all do well."

Jane likes doing jigsaw puzzles. Here she is at the table with a jigsaw puzzle.

She talks to herself as she makes it. "This blue piece must be a piece of sky," she says. "So it goes here." She puts the blue piece into the picture she is making. She has only three pieces left to fit in. Jane is making the jigsaw puzzle quickly.

Peter is on the floor, having a game with the cat and a toy car. He can make the car go along quickly or slowly. At first he makes it go very slowly by the cat. Then the cat goes along slowly after it. Soon she will jump at the car but Peter will pull the car quickly out of her way. Then he will make it go slowly again. Both Peter and the cat enjoy the game.

After a while Jane comes to play with the cat, and then Peter looks at the jigsaw puzzle Jane has made. It is a picture of a boat, the sea and the blue sky.

Peter and Jane have a new toy cupboard. It is a big empty cupboard, and there is room in it for many of their toys. Here they are at the toy cupboard. Their mother wants them to put their toys away before they go to bed.

Peter puts the kite and balloons up at the top of the cupboard. The building set is in a box and so is the jigsaw puzzle. The motor boat and the aeroplane take up a lot of room.

Jane puts away the picture books, the scrapbooks, the camera and the balls. Then she finds a place for the skipping rope, and the nurse's clothes.

"We must not forget the gun," says Peter.

"No," says Jane, "and here are the cowboy's clothes and the Indian's clothes."

They are glad to have this big cupboard. When all the toys have been put away Jane says, "We must ask Mum to look at what we have been doing."

Their mother sees the cupboard and says, "That's good. Thank you."

New words used in this book

Total number of new words: 111
Average repetition per word: 9